40 Egg Recipes for Home

By: Kelly Johnson

Table of Contents

- Classic Scrambled Eggs
- Perfectly Poached Eggs
- French Omelette with Herbs
- Spanish Tortilla (Potato and Egg Omelette)
- Eggs Benedict
- Deviled Eggs
- Shakshuka
- Egg Fried Rice
- Huevos Rancheros
- Spinach and Feta Stuffed Omelette
- Smoked Salmon and Cream Cheese Scramble
- Egg and Avocado Toast
- Egg Salad Sandwich
- Caprese Egg Muffins
- Eggs in Purgatory
- Mushroom and Swiss Cheese Frittata
- Bacon and Cheddar Egg Casserole
- Asparagus and Parmesan Egg Tart
- Sausage and Spinach Breakfast Burrito
- Mediterranean Egg Cups
- Baked Avocado with Egg
- Japanese Tamago Sushi
- Korean Egg Roll (Gyeran Mari)
- Thai Basil and Chili Fried Eggs
- Turkish Menemen
- Indiana Masala Omelette
- Chinese Egg Drop Soup
- Italian Carbonara
- Greek Spanakopita (Spinach Pie)
- Vietnamese Egg Coffee
- Mexican Chiles Rellenos
- Cajun Shrimp and Grits with a Fried Egg
- Egyptian Ful Medames with Egg
- Lebanese Eggplant and Egg Casserole (Batenjan Mehsheh)
- Dutch Baby Pancake with Lemon and Powdered Sugar

- Egg and Vegetable Stir-Fry
- Southwestern Breakfast Burrito
- Caprese Egg Salad
- Smoky Deviled Eggs
- Japanese Tamagoyaki (Sweet Rolled Omelette)

Classic Scrambled Eggs

Ingredients:

- 4 large eggs
- 2 tablespoons butter
- Salt and pepper to taste
- Optional: Chopped fresh herbs (such as chives or parsley) for garnish

Instructions:

Crack the Eggs:
- Crack the eggs into a bowl. Use fresh eggs for the best flavor and texture.

Whisk the Eggs:
- Whisk the eggs with a fork or a whisk until the yolks and whites are well combined. You can add a pinch of salt and pepper at this stage for seasoning.

Preheat the Pan:
- Place a non-stick skillet over medium-low heat and add the butter. Allow it to melt and coat the bottom of the pan evenly.

Pour in the Eggs:
- Pour the beaten eggs into the preheated pan.

Stir Gently:
- Allow the eggs to set slightly around the edges. Use a spatula to gently stir from the edges toward the center. Continue this process, allowing the uncooked egg to flow to the edges.

Control the Heat:
- Adjust the heat as needed to cook the eggs gently. You want soft, creamy curds, so avoid high heat that might result in rubbery eggs.

Remove from Heat:
- As soon as the eggs are mostly set but still slightly runny, remove the pan from the heat. The residual heat will continue to cook the eggs.

Season and Garnish:
- Season the scrambled eggs with salt and pepper to taste. If desired, sprinkle chopped fresh herbs for added flavor and a pop of color.

Serve Immediately:
- Transfer the scrambled eggs to a plate and serve immediately while they are hot and creamy.

Feel free to customize this recipe by adding cheese, diced vegetables, or other ingredients to suit your taste preferences. Enjoy your classic scrambled eggs!

Perfectly Poached Eggs

Ingredients:

- Fresh eggs (as many as you need)
- Water
- Vinegar (optional)
- Salt and pepper, to taste

Instructions:

Choose Fresh Eggs:
- Fresh eggs with firm whites work best for poaching. The fresher the eggs, the better they will hold their shape.

Prepare a Pan with Water:
- Fill a wide saucepan or deep skillet with about 2-3 inches of water. The wide surface area helps the eggs cook evenly.

Add Vinegar (Optional):
- Optionally, add a splash of vinegar to the water. Vinegar helps coagulate the egg whites faster, resulting in neater poached eggs. Use about 1-2 tablespoons of vinegar per quart of water.

Bring Water to a Simmer:
- Heat the water over medium heat until it reaches a gentle simmer. You should see small bubbles forming at the bottom of the pan.

Crack Eggs Into Bowls:
- Crack each egg into a small bowl or ramekin. This makes it easier to slide the egg into the simmering water.

Create a Whirlpool (Optional):
- Swirl the simmering water gently with a spoon to create a whirlpool effect. This helps the egg whites wrap around the yolk for a neater appearance.

Slide Eggs into Water:
- Carefully lower each egg into the simmering water, one at a time. Allow the eggs to slide in gently to avoid breaking the yolks.

Poach Eggs:
- Let the eggs poach for about 3-4 minutes for a soft, runny yolk or longer if you prefer a firmer yolk. The whites should be set, but the yolks should remain runny.

Remove Eggs with a Slotted Spoon:

- Use a slotted spoon to lift the poached eggs out of the water. Allow excess water to drain through the spoon's slots.

Season and Serve:
- Place the poached eggs on a plate, season with salt and pepper, and serve immediately. Enjoy your perfectly poached eggs on toast, English muffins, or with your favorite accompaniments.

Poached eggs are versatile and can be enjoyed in various dishes, such as Eggs Benedict or simply on their own.

French Omelette with Herbs

Ingredients:

- 3 large eggs
- 2 tablespoons unsalted butter
- Salt and pepper to taste
- 2 tablespoons fresh herbs (such as chives, parsley, or tarragon), chopped

Instructions:

Prepare Ingredients:
- Crack the eggs into a bowl, and beat them with a fork or whisk until well combined. Chop the fresh herbs.

Preheat Pan:
- Place a non-stick skillet over medium-low heat. Add 1 tablespoon of butter and let it melt, ensuring it coats the bottom of the pan evenly.

Whisk Eggs:
- Season the beaten eggs with salt and pepper. Whisk the eggs again briefly just before pouring them into the pan.

Pour Eggs into Pan:
- Pour the beaten eggs into the preheated pan. Allow them to set slightly around the edges.

Swirl and Cook Gently:
- With a rubber spatula, gently stir the eggs from the edges toward the center, allowing the uncooked eggs to flow to the edges. Tilt the pan to let the uncooked eggs fill any gaps.

Add Herbs:
- Sprinkle the chopped fresh herbs evenly over the eggs while they are still slightly runny.

Continue Cooking:
- Continue to cook the omelette, lifting the edges with the spatula to let the uncooked egg flow underneath. Cook until the bottom is set but the top is still slightly runny.

Fold and Plate:
- Once the omelette is mostly set but still a little runny on top, fold it in half using the spatula. Slide the omelette onto a plate, folding it as it comes out of the pan.

Add Finishing Touch:

- Add a small pat of butter on top of the folded omelette for extra richness.

Serve Immediately:
- Serve the French omelette hot, and garnish with additional fresh herbs if desired. Enjoy it with a side salad, bread, or your favorite accompaniments.

A French omelette is known for its delicate texture and creamy interior, so take care not to overcook it. Experiment with different herbs to find your favorite flavor combination!

Spanish Tortilla (Potato and Egg Omelette)

Ingredients:

- 4 medium-sized potatoes, peeled and thinly sliced
- 1 large onion, thinly sliced
- 6 large eggs
- Salt and pepper to taste
- 1 cup olive oil (for frying)
- Optional: Chopped fresh parsley for garnish

Instructions:

Prep Potatoes and Onions:
- Peel and thinly slice the potatoes and onions. Pat them dry with a paper towel to remove excess moisture.

Heat Olive Oil:
- In a large skillet, heat the olive oil over medium heat. Add the sliced potatoes and onions, cooking until the potatoes are tender but not browned. This can take around 10-15 minutes. Stir occasionally.

Drain Excess Oil:
- Once the potatoes and onions are cooked, use a slotted spoon to transfer them to a plate lined with paper towels to drain excess oil.

Prepare Egg Mixture:
- In a large mixing bowl, beat the eggs and season with salt and pepper. Add the drained potatoes and onions to the eggs, gently stirring to combine.

Cook the Tortilla:
- In the same skillet, remove most of the excess oil, leaving about 2 tablespoons. Heat the skillet over medium heat. Pour the egg and potato mixture into the skillet.

Cook and Flip:
- Allow the tortilla to cook for about 5-7 minutes or until the edges start to set. Carefully lift the edges with a spatula to check the bottom. Once the bottom is golden brown, it's time to flip.

Use a Plate to Flip:
- Place a large plate upside down over the skillet. Hold the plate and skillet together and flip them to transfer the tortilla onto the plate.

Cook the Other Side:

- Slide the tortilla back into the skillet, uncooked side down. Cook for an additional 5-7 minutes until the entire tortilla is set and golden brown.

Garnish and Serve:
- Once cooked through, slide the Spanish Tortilla onto a serving plate. Optionally, sprinkle chopped fresh parsley on top for garnish.

Serve Warm or at Room Temperature:
- Allow the tortilla to cool slightly before slicing into wedges. It can be served warm or at room temperature.

Spanish Tortilla is a versatile dish that can be served as a tapa, a side dish, or even in a sandwich. Enjoy this flavorful and comforting dish!

Eggs Benedict

Ingredients:

For the Hollandaise Sauce:

- 3 large egg yolks
- 1 tablespoon water
- 1 tablespoon lemon juice
- 1 cup unsalted butter, melted
- Salt and cayenne pepper to taste

For the Eggs Benedict:

- 4 English muffins, split and toasted
- 8 slices Canadian bacon or ham
- 8 large eggs
- Salt and pepper to taste
- Chopped fresh chives or parsley for garnish (optional)

Instructions:

1. Prepare the Hollandaise Sauce:

a. In a heatproof bowl, whisk together egg yolks, water, and lemon juice.

b. Place the bowl over a pot of simmering water (double boiler) and continue whisking until the mixture thickens.

2. Add Melted Butter:

- Slowly drizzle in the melted butter while whisking continuously until the sauce has a smooth and creamy consistency. Season with salt and cayenne pepper to taste. Keep the sauce warm over low heat or in a thermos.

3. Poach the Eggs:

a. Fill a large pan with water and bring it to a gentle simmer.

b. Crack each egg into a small bowl or ramekin.

c. Create a gentle whirlpool in the simmering water and slide the eggs, one at a time, into the center of the whirlpool. Poach for about 3-4 minutes for a runny yolk or longer if you prefer a firmer yolk.

4. Cook Canadian Bacon:

- In a separate skillet, cook the Canadian bacon or ham slices until they are heated through.

5. Assemble the Eggs Benedict:

a. Place toasted English muffin halves on a plate.

b. Top each half with a slice of Canadian bacon.

c. Gently place a poached egg on top of each Canadian bacon slice.

d. Spoon hollandaise sauce generously over each poached egg.

6. Garnish and Serve:

- Optionally, garnish with chopped fresh chives or parsley. Serve immediately while warm.

Enjoy your homemade Eggs Benedict for a delicious and indulgent brunch!

Deviled Eggs

Ingredients:

- 6 large eggs, hard-boiled and peeled
- 1/4 cup mayonnaise
- 1 teaspoon Dijon mustard
- 1 teaspoon white vinegar
- Salt and pepper to taste
- Paprika, for garnish
- Optional: Chopped fresh chives or parsley for garnish

Instructions:

Hard-Boil the Eggs:
- Place the eggs in a single layer in a saucepan and cover with water. Bring to a boil, then reduce the heat and simmer for 10-12 minutes. Remove from heat, drain, and cool the eggs in ice water. Once cooled, peel the eggs.

Slice the Eggs:
- Cut the peeled eggs in half lengthwise. Carefully remove the yolks and place them in a bowl. Arrange the egg white halves on a serving platter.

Make the Filling:
- Mash the egg yolks with a fork. Add mayonnaise, Dijon mustard, white vinegar, salt, and pepper. Mix until smooth and well combined.

Fill the Egg Whites:
- Spoon or pipe the yolk mixture back into the egg white halves. You can use a pastry bag or a zip-top bag with the corner snipped off for a neater presentation.

Garnish:
- Sprinkle paprika over the filled eggs for color and flavor. Optionally, garnish with chopped fresh chives or parsley.

Chill and Serve:
- Refrigerate the deviled eggs for at least 30 minutes before serving to allow the flavors to meld. Serve chilled.

Deviled eggs are versatile, and you can customize the filling with ingredients like chopped pickles, hot sauce, or finely chopped herbs to suit your taste. They make a delightful addition to any party or gathering.

Shakshuka

Ingredients:

- 2 tablespoons olive oil
- 1 onion, finely chopped
- 1 red bell pepper, diced
- 2 garlic cloves, minced
- 1 teaspoon ground cumin
- 1 teaspoon smoked paprika
- 1/2 teaspoon ground coriander
- 1/4 teaspoon cayenne pepper (optional, for heat)
- 1 can (28 ounces) crushed tomatoes
- Salt and pepper to taste
- 4-6 large eggs
- Chopped fresh cilantro or parsley for garnish
- Feta cheese (optional, for garnish)
- Crusty bread or pita for serving

Instructions:

Prepare the Sauce:
- Heat olive oil in a large, deep skillet or sauté pan over medium heat. Add chopped onions and diced red bell pepper. Cook until softened, about 5-7 minutes.

Add Aromatics and Spices:
- Add minced garlic, ground cumin, smoked paprika, ground coriander, and cayenne pepper (if using). Stir and cook for another 1-2 minutes until fragrant.

Tomato Base:
- Pour in the crushed tomatoes, and season with salt and pepper to taste. Simmer the sauce for about 10-15 minutes, allowing it to thicken.

Make Wells for Eggs:
- Using a spoon, make small wells in the sauce for each egg. Crack an egg into each well.

Poach the Eggs:

- Cover the skillet and let the eggs poach in the simmering sauce for about 5-7 minutes or until the egg whites are set but the yolks are still runny. You can cook them longer if you prefer a firmer yolk.

Garnish:
- Sprinkle chopped cilantro or parsley over the top. If desired, crumble feta cheese on top for added flavor.

Serve:
- Serve the shakshuka directly from the skillet. Scoop out eggs with some sauce onto plates. Enjoy with crusty bread or pita for dipping.

Shakshuka is a perfect brunch or dinner dish, and its rich, savory flavors make it a comforting and satisfying meal.

Egg Fried Rice

Ingredients:

- 3 cups cooked and cooled jasmine or basmati rice (preferably a day old)
- 2 tablespoons vegetable oil
- 2 large eggs, lightly beaten
- 1 cup mixed vegetables (peas, carrots, corn, and diced bell peppers)
- 3 green onions, thinly sliced
- 3 cloves garlic, minced
- 2 tablespoons soy sauce
- 1 tablespoon oyster sauce (optional)
- 1 teaspoon sesame oil
- Salt and pepper to taste

Instructions:

Prep Ingredients:
- Ensure that all your ingredients are prepared and ready to go before you start cooking. Having everything ready will make the cooking process smooth and quick.

Heat the Pan:
- Heat a large skillet or wok over medium-high heat. Add 1 tablespoon of vegetable oil.

Scramble the Eggs:
- Pour the beaten eggs into the hot pan. Allow them to cook undisturbed for a moment, then scramble them with a spatula. Once cooked, transfer the scrambled eggs to a plate and set aside.

Cook Vegetables:
- In the same pan, add the remaining tablespoon of oil. Add minced garlic and stir-fry for about 30 seconds until fragrant. Add the mixed vegetables and stir-fry for 2-3 minutes until they are slightly tender but still crisp.

Add Rice:
- Add the cooked and cooled rice to the pan. Break up any clumps and stir-fry for a few minutes until the rice is heated through.

Combine Eggs:
- Return the scrambled eggs to the pan. Mix them into the rice and vegetables.

Season:
- Drizzle soy sauce, oyster sauce (if using), and sesame oil over the rice. Season with salt and pepper to taste. Stir well to combine all the ingredients evenly.

Finish with Green Onions:
- Add sliced green onions to the fried rice. Stir for another minute or until everything is well incorporated.

Serve Hot:
- Transfer the egg fried rice to a serving dish and serve hot. You can garnish with additional green onions if desired.

Enjoy your homemade egg fried rice as a tasty and satisfying meal! You can also customize it by adding cooked chicken, shrimp, or tofu for added protein.

Huevos Rancheros

Ingredients:

- 4 corn tortillas
- 4 large eggs
- 1 cup black beans, cooked and drained
- 1 cup diced tomatoes
- 1/2 cup diced onions
- 1/2 cup diced bell peppers (any color)
- 2 cloves garlic, minced
- 1 jalapeño, seeded and minced (optional, for heat)
- 1 teaspoon ground cumin
- 1 teaspoon smoked paprika
- Salt and pepper to taste
- 1 cup shredded Mexican cheese blend
- Fresh cilantro, chopped, for garnish
- Avocado slices, for serving
- Lime wedges, for serving

Instructions:

Prepare the Tortillas:
- Heat a non-stick skillet over medium heat. Lightly toast the corn tortillas on both sides until they are warm and pliable. Set aside.

Cook the Sauce:
- In the same skillet, add a bit of oil if needed. Saute diced onions, bell peppers, and garlic until softened. Add diced tomatoes and jalapeño (if using), and cook until the tomatoes release their juices.

Season the Sauce:
- Stir in ground cumin, smoked paprika, salt, and pepper. Cook for an additional 5-7 minutes until the sauce thickens slightly.

Prepare the Eggs:
- In a separate pan, cook the eggs to your liking (fried or poached).

Assemble the Dish:
- Place the toasted tortillas on plates. Spread a spoonful of black beans over each tortilla. Place a fried egg on top of the beans.

Top with Sauce and Cheese:

- Spoon the tomato-chili sauce over each egg. Sprinkle shredded Mexican cheese over the top.

Garnish:
- Garnish with fresh cilantro and serve with avocado slices on the side.

Serve Hot:
- Serve Huevos Rancheros immediately, with lime wedges on the side for squeezing over the top.

Enjoy this flavorful and hearty Mexican breakfast dish! Huevos Rancheros is a satisfying meal that combines bold flavors and textures, making it a great start to your day.

Spinach and Feta Stuffed Omelette

Ingredients:

- 3 large eggs
- 1 cup fresh spinach, chopped
- 1/4 cup crumbled feta cheese
- 1/4 cup diced tomatoes
- 1/4 cup diced red onions
- 1 clove garlic, minced
- Salt and pepper to taste
- 1 tablespoon olive oil or butter
- Fresh herbs (such as dill or parsley) for garnish (optional)

Instructions:

Prepare the Filling:
- In a bowl, mix together chopped spinach, crumbled feta cheese, diced tomatoes, diced red onions, and minced garlic. Set aside.

Beat the Eggs:
- Crack the eggs into a bowl, add a pinch of salt and pepper, and beat them with a fork or whisk until well combined.

Cook the Filling:
- Heat olive oil or butter in a non-stick skillet over medium heat. Add the spinach and feta filling mixture to the skillet and sauté for 2-3 minutes until the spinach wilts and the ingredients are well combined. Remove the mixture from the skillet and set it aside.

Cook the Omelette:
- In the same skillet, add a bit more oil or butter if needed. Pour the beaten eggs into the skillet and let them set for a moment.

Add the Filling:
- Spoon the spinach and feta filling onto one half of the omelette.

Fold and Cook:
- Carefully fold the other half of the omelette over the filling, creating a half-moon shape. Allow it to cook for an additional 1-2 minutes until the eggs are fully cooked.

Garnish and Serve:
- Slide the omelette onto a plate, garnish with fresh herbs if desired, and serve hot.

This Spinach and Feta Stuffed Omelette is not only delicious but also packed with protein and nutrients. Customize it by adding other vegetables or herbs to suit your taste preferences. Enjoy your wholesome and flavorful breakfast!

Smoked Salmon and Cream Cheese Scramble

Ingredients:

- 4 large eggs
- 2 tablespoons cream cheese, softened
- 2 ounces smoked salmon, chopped
- 1 tablespoon chives, finely chopped
- Salt and pepper to taste
- 1 tablespoon butter
- Optional: Lemon wedges and additional chives for garnish
- Toast or bagels, for serving

Instructions:

Prepare Ingredients:
- Crack the eggs into a bowl, add the softened cream cheese, and whisk together until well combined. Stir in the chopped smoked salmon and chives. Season with salt and pepper to taste.

Heat Butter:
- Heat the butter in a non-stick skillet over medium heat until it starts to sizzle.

Scramble Eggs:
- Pour the egg mixture into the skillet. Allow the eggs to set slightly around the edges, and then gently stir with a spatula, folding the eggs over themselves.

Add Smoked Salmon:
- As the eggs continue to cook, add the chopped smoked salmon to the pan, ensuring it is evenly distributed throughout the scramble.

Continue Cooking:
- Continue to cook the eggs, stirring gently, until they are cooked to your desired level of doneness. The cream cheese will melt into the eggs, creating a creamy and luxurious texture.

Adjust Seasoning:
- Taste the scramble and adjust the seasoning with additional salt and pepper if needed.

Garnish and Serve:
- Once the eggs are cooked, transfer the scramble to a plate. Garnish with additional chives and serve with lemon wedges on the side.

Serve with Toast or Bagels:
- Toast slices of bread or serve with toasted bagels on the side. The creamy and savory smoked salmon and cream cheese scramble pairs wonderfully with the toasty texture of bread.

Enjoy this decadent and flavorful breakfast with the combination of smoked salmon and rich cream cheese, creating a luxurious start to your day!

Egg and Avocado Toast

Ingredients:

- 2 slices of whole-grain bread (or your preferred bread)
- 1 ripe avocado
- 2 large eggs
- Salt and pepper to taste
- Red pepper flakes (optional, for added spice)
- Olive oil (for drizzling, optional)
- Fresh herbs (such as chives, parsley, or cilantro) for garnish

Instructions:

Toast the Bread:
- Toast the slices of bread to your preferred level of crispiness.

Prepare the Avocado:
- While the bread is toasting, cut the ripe avocado in half, remove the pit, and scoop the flesh into a bowl. Mash the avocado with a fork and season it with salt and pepper to taste. If you like, you can add a dash of red pepper flakes for a bit of spice.

Cook the Eggs:
- Cook the eggs to your liking. You can prepare them as fried eggs, poached eggs, or scrambled eggs. Season with salt and pepper.

Assemble the Toast:
- Spread the mashed avocado evenly over the toasted bread slices.

Top with Eggs:
- Place the cooked eggs on top of the mashed avocado.

Drizzle with Olive Oil (Optional):
- If desired, drizzle a little olive oil over the eggs for extra richness.

Garnish:
- Garnish the toast with fresh herbs of your choice, such as chopped chives, parsley, or cilantro.

Serve Immediately:
- Enjoy your egg and avocado toast immediately while it's warm.

This simple and nutritious Egg and Avocado Toast makes for a satisfying and flavorful meal. It's a great way to start your day with a balance of protein, healthy fats, and whole grains.

Egg Salad Sandwich

Ingredients:

- 6 hard-boiled eggs, peeled and chopped
- 1/4 cup mayonnaise
- 1 tablespoon Dijon mustard
- 1 celery stalk, finely diced
- 2 tablespoons red onion, finely chopped
- Salt and pepper to taste
- Fresh chives or parsley, chopped (optional)
- Bread slices or rolls for making sandwiches
- Lettuce leaves and tomato slices for garnish (optional)

Instructions:

Prepare the Eggs:
- Hard-boil the eggs and let them cool. Peel the eggs and chop them into small pieces.

Make the Egg Salad:
- In a bowl, combine the chopped eggs, mayonnaise, Dijon mustard, diced celery, and chopped red onion. Mix until all ingredients are well combined.

Season:
- Season the egg salad with salt and pepper to taste. You can also add chopped fresh chives or parsley for added flavor.

Assemble the Sandwich:
- Place a generous scoop of the egg salad onto a slice of bread. If you prefer, you can lightly toast the bread beforehand.

Add Garnishes (Optional):
- Top the egg salad with lettuce leaves, tomato slices, or any other garnishes of your choice.

Complete the Sandwich:
- Place another slice of bread on top to complete the sandwich.

Serve:
- Cut the sandwich in half if desired and serve immediately.

Feel free to customize the egg salad by adding ingredients like diced pickles, capers, or a dash of hot sauce for extra flavor. Egg salad sandwiches are versatile and perfect for picnics, lunches, or a quick and easy meal at home.

Caprese Egg Muffins

Ingredients:

- 6 large eggs
- 1/2 cup cherry tomatoes, diced
- 1/2 cup fresh mozzarella, diced
- 2 tablespoons fresh basil, chopped
- Salt and pepper to taste
- Olive oil for greasing the muffin tin

Instructions:

Preheat the Oven:
- Preheat your oven to 350°F (175°C).

Prepare the Muffin Tin:
- Lightly grease a muffin tin with olive oil to prevent sticking.

Prepare the Ingredients:
- Dice the cherry tomatoes and fresh mozzarella. Chop the fresh basil.

Whisk the Eggs:
- In a bowl, whisk the eggs until well beaten. Season with salt and pepper to taste.

Combine Ingredients:
- Add the diced cherry tomatoes, fresh mozzarella, and chopped basil to the beaten eggs. Mix well to combine.

Fill the Muffin Cups:
- Pour the egg mixture evenly into the greased muffin tin, filling each cup about two-thirds full.

Bake:
- Bake in the preheated oven for approximately 15-18 minutes or until the eggs are set and a toothpick inserted into the center comes out clean.

Cool and Serve:
- Allow the Caprese Egg Muffins to cool for a few minutes in the muffin tin. Use a butter knife to gently loosen the edges and remove the muffins.

Garnish (Optional):
- Garnish with additional fresh basil if desired.

Serve Warm or at Room Temperature:
- Serve the Caprese Egg Muffins warm or at room temperature.

These Caprese Egg Muffins are a delightful and portable breakfast or snack. They're perfect for those who enjoy the classic combination of tomatoes, mozzarella, and basil. Enjoy these tasty and protein-packed muffins!

Eggs in Purgatory

Ingredients:

- 2 tablespoons olive oil
- 1 small onion, finely chopped
- 2 cloves garlic, minced
- 1 can (14 oz) crushed tomatoes
- 1 teaspoon red pepper flakes (adjust to taste for spiciness)
- Salt and pepper to taste
- 4-6 large eggs
- Fresh basil or parsley, chopped, for garnish
- Grated Parmesan or Pecorino cheese (optional, for serving)
- Crusty bread, for serving

Instructions:

Prepare the Sauce:
- In a large skillet or pan, heat olive oil over medium heat. Add chopped onions and cook until softened, about 3-5 minutes. Add minced garlic and cook for an additional 1-2 minutes until fragrant.

Add Tomatoes and Spices:
- Pour in the crushed tomatoes, red pepper flakes, salt, and pepper. Stir well to combine. Allow the sauce to simmer for about 10-15 minutes, or until it thickens slightly.

Create Wells for Eggs:
- Make small wells in the sauce using a spoon. Crack each egg into a small bowl, then gently slide each egg into the wells you created in the sauce.

Poach the Eggs:
- Cover the skillet and let the eggs poach in the simmering tomato sauce for about 5-7 minutes or until the egg whites are set, and the yolks are still runny. Cook longer if you prefer firmer yolks.

Garnish:
- Sprinkle fresh basil or parsley over the eggs for garnish.

Serve:
- Serve the Eggs in Purgatory hot directly from the skillet. Optionally, sprinkle with grated Parmesan or Pecorino cheese. Provide crusty bread for dipping.

This dish is not only delicious but also easy to customize. You can add other ingredients like bell peppers, black olives, or even crumbled sausage to enhance the flavor. Enjoy your Eggs in Purgatory with the runny yolks mingling with the spicy tomato sauce!

Mushroom and Swiss Cheese Frittata

Ingredients:

- 8 large eggs
- 1/4 cup milk or cream
- Salt and pepper to taste
- 2 tablespoons olive oil
- 1 small onion, finely chopped
- 8 ounces mushrooms, sliced
- 1 cup Swiss cheese, shredded
- 2 tablespoons fresh parsley, chopped (for garnish)

Instructions:

Preheat the Oven:
- Preheat your oven to 375°F (190°C).

Prepare Ingredients:
- Beat the eggs in a bowl, add milk or cream, and season with salt and pepper. Whisk the mixture until well combined. Chop the onion, slice the mushrooms, and shred the Swiss cheese.

Sauté Mushrooms and Onions:
- Heat olive oil in an oven-safe skillet over medium heat. Add chopped onions and sliced mushrooms. Cook until the mushrooms release their moisture and the onions are softened, about 5-7 minutes.

Add Eggs and Cheese:
- Pour the beaten egg mixture over the sautéed mushrooms and onions in the skillet. Allow it to set for a minute or two.

Swirl and Cook Gently:
- Gently swirl the egg mixture around the skillet, allowing the uncooked eggs to flow to the edges. Sprinkle shredded Swiss cheese evenly over the top.

Transfer to the Oven:
- Transfer the skillet to the preheated oven and bake for about 12-15 minutes, or until the frittata is set in the center and the edges are golden brown.

Garnish and Serve:
- Remove the frittata from the oven. Garnish with fresh chopped parsley.

Slice and Serve:

- Allow the frittata to cool slightly, then slice it into wedges. Serve warm.

This Mushroom and Swiss Cheese Frittata is not only delicious but also versatile. You can customize it by adding other ingredients such as spinach, bell peppers, or herbs. Enjoy this savory and satisfying dish for any meal of the day!

Bacon and Cheddar Egg Casserole

Ingredients:

- 8 large eggs
- 1 cup milk
- 6 slices bacon, cooked and crumbled
- 1 cup shredded cheddar cheese
- 1/2 cup diced onions
- 1/2 cup diced bell peppers (any color)
- 1/2 cup diced tomatoes
- 1/4 cup chopped fresh parsley
- Salt and pepper to taste
- Cooking spray or butter for greasing the baking dish

Instructions:

Preheat the Oven:
- Preheat your oven to 350°F (175°C).

Prepare Ingredients:
- Cook the bacon until crispy, then crumble it. Dice the onions, bell peppers, and tomatoes. Shred the cheddar cheese.

Grease the Baking Dish:
- Grease a 9x13-inch baking dish with cooking spray or butter.

Assemble the Casserole:
- In a large bowl, whisk together the eggs and milk. Add the crumbled bacon, shredded cheddar cheese, diced onions, bell peppers, tomatoes, and chopped parsley. Season with salt and pepper to taste. Mix well to combine.

Pour into Baking Dish:
- Pour the egg mixture into the prepared baking dish, spreading it evenly.

Bake:
- Bake in the preheated oven for about 25-30 minutes or until the eggs are set in the center and the top is golden brown.

Cool and Serve:
- Allow the casserole to cool for a few minutes before slicing it into squares or rectangles. Serve warm.

Garnish (Optional):

- Garnish with additional chopped parsley, if desired.

This Bacon and Cheddar Egg Casserole is not only easy to make but also versatile. Feel free to customize it by adding other ingredients like spinach, mushrooms, or different types of cheese. It's a fantastic dish for feeding a crowd or for meal prep, as it can be made ahead of time and reheated when needed. Enjoy!

Asparagus and Parmesan Egg Tart

Ingredients:

For the Tart Crust:

- 1 1/4 cups all-purpose flour
- 1/2 cup unsalted butter, chilled and diced
- 1/4 teaspoon salt
- 3-4 tablespoons ice water

For the Filling:

- 1 bunch asparagus, trimmed
- 4 large eggs
- 1/2 cup heavy cream
- 1/2 cup grated Parmesan cheese
- Salt and pepper to taste
- Fresh parsley, chopped, for garnish (optional)

Instructions:

1. Prepare the Tart Crust:

- In a food processor, pulse the flour, chilled diced butter, and salt until the mixture resembles coarse crumbs.
- Add ice water, one tablespoon at a time, and pulse until the dough comes together.
- Shape the dough into a disc, wrap it in plastic wrap, and refrigerate for at least 30 minutes.

2. Preheat the Oven:

- Preheat your oven to 375°F (190°C).

3. Roll out the Tart Crust:

- On a lightly floured surface, roll out the chilled dough into a circle large enough to fit into a tart pan. Press the dough into the pan, trim the excess, and prick the bottom with a fork. Line the crust with parchment paper and fill it with pie weights or dried beans.

4. Blind Bake the Crust:

- Bake the crust in the preheated oven for about 15 minutes. Remove the parchment paper and weights, then bake for an additional 5 minutes or until the crust is golden brown.

5. Prepare the Filling:

- While the crust is baking, blanch the trimmed asparagus in boiling water for 2-3 minutes, then transfer to an ice bath to stop the cooking. Cut the asparagus into smaller pieces.
- In a bowl, whisk together eggs, heavy cream, grated Parmesan cheese, salt, and pepper.

6. Assemble and Bake:

- Arrange the blanched asparagus pieces on the partially baked tart crust. Pour the egg and cream mixture over the asparagus.
- Bake in the oven for 20-25 minutes or until the filling is set and golden brown.

7. Garnish and Serve:

- Remove the tart from the oven and let it cool for a few minutes. Garnish with fresh chopped parsley if desired.

8. Slice and Enjoy:

- Slice the Asparagus and Parmesan Egg Tart into wedges and serve warm.

This elegant tart is a delightful combination of the earthy flavor of asparagus and the richness of Parmesan. It's perfect for special occasions or when you want to impress your guests with a visually stunning and delicious dish.

Sausage and Spinach Breakfast Burrito

Ingredients:

- 4 large eggs
- 1/2 pound breakfast sausage, casings removed
- 2 cups fresh spinach, chopped
- 1 cup shredded cheddar cheese
- 4 large flour tortillas
- Salt and pepper to taste
- Salsa or hot sauce for serving (optional)
- Chopped fresh cilantro or green onions for garnish (optional)

Instructions:

Cook the Sausage:
- In a skillet over medium heat, cook the breakfast sausage, breaking it apart with a spatula, until browned and cooked through. Remove excess grease if necessary.

Add Spinach:
- Add the chopped spinach to the skillet with the cooked sausage. Cook for an additional 2-3 minutes or until the spinach wilts.

Scramble the Eggs:
- Push the sausage and spinach to one side of the skillet. Crack the eggs into the empty side and scramble them. Once the eggs are almost set, mix them with the sausage and spinach. Season with salt and pepper to taste.

Assemble the Burritos:
- Warm the flour tortillas in a dry skillet or microwave. Place a portion of the sausage, spinach, and scrambled eggs mixture onto each tortilla. Sprinkle shredded cheddar cheese over the top.

Fold and Roll:
- Fold the sides of the tortilla inwards and then roll it up tightly from the bottom to create a burrito.

Serve:
- Place the breakfast burritos seam-side down on a serving plate. If desired, garnish with chopped cilantro or green onions.

Optional: Add Salsa or Hot Sauce:
- Serve the breakfast burritos with salsa or hot sauce on the side for extra flavor.

Enjoy your Sausage and Spinach Breakfast Burrito as a convenient and delicious morning meal. You can also customize the filling by adding ingredients like diced tomatoes, avocados, or black beans to suit your taste preferences.

Mediterranean Egg Cups

Ingredients:

- 6 large eggs
- 1/2 cup cherry tomatoes, diced
- 1/4 cup Kalamata olives, chopped
- 1/4 cup feta cheese, crumbled
- 2 tablespoons fresh parsley, chopped
- 1 tablespoon olive oil
- Salt and pepper to taste
- Optional: Red pepper flakes for added heat
- Cooking spray or olive oil for greasing the muffin tin

Instructions:

Preheat the Oven:
- Preheat your oven to 375°F (190°C).

Prepare the Muffin Tin:
- Grease a 6-cup muffin tin with cooking spray or a small amount of olive oil.

Assemble the Egg Cups:
- In each muffin cup, add a small drizzle of olive oil. Crack an egg into each cup.

Add Toppings:
- Sprinkle diced cherry tomatoes, chopped Kalamata olives, crumbled feta cheese, and chopped parsley over each egg. Season with salt and pepper to taste.

Bake:
- Bake in the preheated oven for approximately 12-15 minutes or until the egg whites are set, and the yolks are cooked to your liking.

Optional: Add Heat:
- If you like a bit of heat, sprinkle red pepper flakes over the egg cups before baking.

Garnish:
- Once baked, garnish with additional fresh parsley if desired.

Serve Warm:
- Allow the Mediterranean Egg Cups to cool for a few minutes before serving. Serve warm.

These Mediterranean Egg Cups are not only delicious but also versatile. You can customize them by adding ingredients like spinach, sun-dried tomatoes, or diced bell peppers. Enjoy this Mediterranean-inspired breakfast for a flavorful and protein-packed start to your day!

Baked Avocado with Egg

Ingredients:

- 2 ripe avocados
- 4 large eggs
- Salt and pepper to taste
- Optional toppings: chopped fresh herbs (such as cilantro, parsley, or chives), grated cheese, cooked bacon or sausage crumbles, hot sauce, or salsa

Instructions:

Preheat the Oven:
- Preheat your oven to 375°F (190°C).

Prepare the Avocados:
- Cut each avocado in half lengthwise and remove the pit. Use a spoon to scoop out a bit of flesh from each avocado half to create a larger cavity for the egg.

Create a Stable Base:
- If needed, slice a small portion off the rounded bottom of each avocado half to create a stable base so they sit flat on a baking dish.

Crack Eggs into Avocado Halves:
- Place the avocado halves in a baking dish or on a baking sheet lined with parchment paper. Crack one egg into each avocado half, allowing the egg white to fill the cavity. If the avocado halves are small, you may need to scoop out a bit more flesh to accommodate the egg.

Season:
- Season the eggs with salt and pepper to taste, and any other desired seasonings or toppings.

Bake:
- Carefully transfer the baking dish to the preheated oven and bake for about 15-20 minutes, or until the egg whites are set and the yolks are cooked to your desired level of doneness. Keep an eye on them as baking times may vary depending on the size of your avocados and eggs.

Garnish and Serve:
- Once baked, remove the avocado and egg halves from the oven. Garnish with your favorite toppings such as chopped fresh herbs, grated cheese, cooked bacon or sausage crumbles, hot sauce, or salsa. Serve immediately.

This Baked Avocado with Egg dish is not only delicious but also packed with healthy fats, protein, and nutrients. It makes for a satisfying breakfast, brunch, or light meal any time of the day. Feel free to customize it with your favorite ingredients and enjoy!

Japanese Tamago Sushi

Ingredients:

For the Tamago (Sweet Omelet):

- 4 large eggs
- 2 tablespoons sugar
- 1 tablespoon soy sauce
- 1 tablespoon mirin (Japanese sweet rice wine)
- 1/2 teaspoon salt
- Cooking oil for greasing the pan

For the Sushi Rice:

- 2 cups sushi rice
- 1/4 cup rice vinegar
- 2 tablespoons sugar
- 1 teaspoon salt

For Assembling Tamago Sushi:

- Nori (seaweed) sheets, cut into thin strips (optional)
- Soy sauce for dipping
- Pickled ginger and wasabi for serving (optional)

Instructions:

1. Prepare Sushi Rice:

- Rinse the sushi rice under cold water until the water runs clear. Cook the rice according to the package instructions.
- While the rice is still hot, gently mix it with rice vinegar, sugar, and salt. Allow the rice to cool to room temperature.

2. Make the Tamago (Sweet Omelet):

- In a bowl, whisk together eggs, sugar, soy sauce, mirin, and salt until well combined.

- Heat a square or rectangular tamago pan or a non-stick skillet over medium heat. Lightly grease the pan with cooking oil.
- Pour a thin layer of the egg mixture into the pan, allowing it to set slightly. Roll the set layer to one side of the pan, leaving space to pour another thin layer of the egg mixture. Repeat until all the egg mixture is used.
- Roll the layers into a log shape and transfer it to a bamboo sushi rolling mat. Wrap the mat around the tamago log and squeeze gently to shape it. Allow it to cool.

3. Assemble Tamago Sushi:

- Cut the tamago log into thin slices.
- Wet your hands with water and shape small portions of sushi rice into oblong-shaped mounds.
- Place a slice of tamago on top of each rice mound.
- Optionally, you can wrap a thin strip of nori around the sushi to secure the tamago in place.

4. Serve:

- Arrange the Tamago Sushi on a serving plate.
- Serve with soy sauce for dipping and, if desired, pickled ginger and wasabi.

Enjoy the sweet and savory flavors of Tamago Sushi! It's a delightful addition to any sushi platter and a popular choice in Japanese cuisine.

Korean Egg Roll (Gyeran Mari)

Ingredients:

- 4 large eggs
- 2 tablespoons milk
- 1/4 teaspoon salt
- 1 tablespoon vegetable oil
- 2 green onions, finely chopped
- 1/4 cup carrot, julienned
- Salt and pepper to taste
- Sesame oil (optional, for flavor)
- Roasted sesame seeds (optional, for garnish)

Instructions:

Prepare Vegetables:
- Finely chop the green onions and julienne the carrot.

Whisk Eggs:
- In a bowl, whisk the eggs. Add milk, salt, and whisk until well combined.

Sauté Vegetables:
- Heat vegetable oil in a non-stick skillet over medium heat. Add green onions and carrots. Sauté until the vegetables are softened, about 2-3 minutes. Season with salt and pepper.

Add Whisked Eggs:
- Push the sautéed vegetables to one side of the skillet. Pour the whisked eggs into the empty side of the skillet. Let it set for a moment.

Roll the Egg:
- Once the edges of the egg start to set, roll it from one side to the other, creating a log or roll shape. Push the rolled portion to the side and add more egg mixture to the empty side. Lift the rolled portion to let the uncooked egg flow underneath.

Continue Rolling:
- Repeat the process of rolling and adding more egg mixture until all the egg is used. This creates layers in the egg roll.

Shape and Cook:
- Continue rolling the egg roll to form a tight log. You can shape the roll by pressing gently with a spatula or by using a bamboo sushi rolling mat. Cook until the egg is fully set and cooked through.

Slice and Serve:
- Allow the egg roll to cool slightly, then slice it into rounds. Drizzle with a bit of sesame oil for flavor and sprinkle with roasted sesame seeds if desired.

Serve Warm or at Room Temperature:
- Korean Egg Roll can be served warm or at room temperature. It makes a great side dish, snack, or part of a Korean-style meal.

Enjoy the savory and slightly sweet flavors of Korean Egg Roll (Gyeran Mari)! It's a versatile dish that can be customized with different vegetables and seasonings to suit your taste.

Thai Basil and Chili Fried Eggs

Ingredients:

- 4 large eggs
- 2 tablespoons vegetable oil
- 4 cloves garlic, minced
- 2-3 red bird's eye chilies, finely chopped (adjust to your spice preference)
- 1 cup fresh Thai basil leaves, loosely packed
- 1 tablespoon oyster sauce
- 1 tablespoon soy sauce
- 1 teaspoon fish sauce
- 1 teaspoon sugar
- Lime wedges for serving
- Jasmine rice for serving

Instructions:

Prepare Ingredients:
- Whisk the eggs in a bowl and set aside. Mince the garlic, chop the red chilies, and have the Thai basil leaves ready.

Heat Oil:
- In a large skillet or wok, heat the vegetable oil over medium-high heat.

Sauté Garlic and Chilies:
- Add minced garlic and chopped red chilies to the hot oil. Stir-fry for about 30 seconds until fragrant. Be cautious as the chilies can release a strong aroma.

Add Eggs:
- Pour the whisked eggs into the skillet, spreading them out evenly. Allow the eggs to set for a moment.

Stir-Fry Eggs:
- Gently stir-fry the eggs, breaking them apart into smaller pieces as they cook.

Add Sauces and Sugar:
- Once the eggs are almost fully cooked, add oyster sauce, soy sauce, fish sauce, and sugar. Continue to stir-fry to coat the eggs evenly with the sauces.

Add Thai Basil:

- Add the fresh Thai basil leaves to the eggs and stir until the basil is just wilted. This should only take about 30 seconds to 1 minute.

Taste and Adjust:
- Taste the dish and adjust the seasoning if needed. You can add more soy sauce, fish sauce, or sugar according to your preference.

Serve:
- Transfer the Thai Basil and Chili Fried Eggs to a serving plate. Serve with jasmine rice and lime wedges on the side.

Enjoy:
- Squeeze lime juice over the eggs before eating to enhance the flavors.

This Thai street food-inspired dish is quick to make and bursts with the aromatic flavors of Thai basil and chilies. It's a perfect combination of spicy, savory, and aromatic elements. Enjoy your Thai Basil and Chili Fried Eggs with rice for a delightful meal!

Turkish Menemen

Ingredients:

- 2 tablespoons olive oil
- 1 onion, finely chopped
- 2 green bell peppers, thinly sliced
- 2 tomatoes, diced
- 3-4 eggs
- Salt and pepper to taste
- Red pepper flakes (optional, for added heat)
- Fresh parsley, chopped, for garnish
- Feta cheese or Turkish beyaz peynir (optional, for serving)
- Turkish bread or crusty bread, for serving

Instructions:

Prepare Vegetables:
- Heat olive oil in a large skillet over medium heat. Add finely chopped onions and cook until softened.

Add Peppers:
- Add thinly sliced green bell peppers to the skillet. Sauté until the peppers are softened.

Add Tomatoes:
- Add diced tomatoes to the skillet. Cook until the tomatoes release their juices and the mixture becomes somewhat saucy.

Season:
- Season the mixture with salt and pepper to taste. Add red pepper flakes if you want some heat.

Create Wells for Eggs:
- Make small wells or indentations in the vegetable mixture using a spoon. Crack an egg into each well.

Cook Eggs:
- Cover the skillet and let the eggs cook until the whites are set but the yolks are still runny, or cook to your desired level of doneness.

Garnish:
- Sprinkle fresh parsley over the Menemen for added freshness.

Serve:

- Serve Menemen hot directly from the skillet. Optionally, crumble feta cheese or Turkish beyaz peynir over the top.

Enjoy with Bread:
- Enjoy Menemen with Turkish bread or crusty bread for dipping.

Turkish Menemen is a comforting and satisfying dish with the rich flavors of tomatoes, peppers, and eggs. It's often enjoyed with a side of bread for a complete and hearty breakfast or brunch experience.

Indiana Masala Omelette

Ingredients:

- 3 large eggs
- 1 small onion, finely chopped
- 1 small tomato, diced
- 1 green chili, finely chopped (adjust to your spice preference)
- 1/2 teaspoon garam masala
- 1/2 teaspoon cumin powder
- 1/4 teaspoon turmeric powder
- Salt and pepper to taste
- Fresh cilantro, chopped, for garnish
- 2 tablespoons oil or ghee for cooking

Instructions:

Prepare Vegetables:
- In a bowl, mix the finely chopped onion, diced tomato, and chopped green chili.

Whisk Eggs:
- In another bowl, whisk the eggs until well beaten.

Season Eggs:
- Add garam masala, cumin powder, turmeric powder, salt, and pepper to the beaten eggs. Mix well.

Combine Eggs and Vegetables:
- Pour the spiced eggs over the vegetable mixture. Stir to combine everything evenly.

Cook the Omelette:
- Heat oil or ghee in a skillet over medium heat. Pour the egg and vegetable mixture into the skillet.
- Allow the omelette to cook undisturbed for a minute or two until the edges set.
- Gently lift the edges with a spatula to let the uncooked egg flow underneath.
- Continue cooking until the omelette is set but still moist on top.

Fold and Serve:
- Once the omelette is cooked to your liking, fold it in half with a spatula.

Garnish:
- Transfer the omelette to a plate. Garnish with fresh cilantro.

Serve:
- Serve the Indiana Masala Omelette hot, either on its own or with toast.

Feel free to customize this recipe based on your taste preferences. You can add other ingredients like bell peppers, spinach, or cheese for additional flavor. Enjoy your flavorful masala omelette inspired by Indiana!

Chinese Egg Drop Soup

Ingredients:

- 4 cups chicken or vegetable broth
- 1/2 teaspoon grated ginger
- 2 tablespoons soy sauce
- 1 teaspoon sesame oil
- 1/4 teaspoon white pepper (or black pepper)
- 2 green onions, finely chopped
- 2 large eggs, beaten
- 1 tablespoon cornstarch mixed with 2 tablespoons water (optional, for thickening)
- Salt to taste
- Chopped cilantro for garnish (optional)

Instructions:

Prepare Broth:
- In a saucepan, bring the chicken or vegetable broth to a gentle simmer over medium heat.

Add Flavorings:
- Add grated ginger, soy sauce, sesame oil, and white pepper to the simmering broth. Stir well to combine.

Thicken (Optional):
- If you prefer a slightly thicker soup, mix cornstarch with water to make a slurry. Slowly pour the slurry into the simmering broth while stirring continuously. Continue stirring until the soup thickens slightly.

Create Egg Ribbons:
- With the broth still simmering, use a fork or chopsticks to stir the soup in a circular motion. Gradually pour the beaten eggs into the swirling soup in a thin stream. This will create delicate egg ribbons.

Season and Garnish:
- Season the soup with salt to taste. Add chopped green onions and cilantro for garnish.

Serve:
- Ladle the Chinese Egg Drop Soup into bowls and serve immediately.

Enjoy the warmth and simplicity of this classic Chinese soup. It's a great option for a light appetizer or a comforting meal. Feel free to customize the soup by adding ingredients like tofu, mushrooms, or spinach based on your preferences.

Italian Carbonara

Ingredients:

- 400 grams (14 ounces) spaghetti or other pasta
- 150 grams (5 ounces) pancetta or guanciale, diced
- 3 large eggs
- 1 cup Pecorino Romano cheese, grated
- 1/2 cup Parmesan cheese, grated
- Freshly ground black pepper, to taste
- Salt, for pasta water

Instructions:

Prepare Pasta:
- Bring a large pot of salted water to a boil. Cook the spaghetti or pasta according to the package instructions until al dente.

Cook Pancetta or Guanciale:
- While the pasta is cooking, heat a drizzle of olive oil in a skillet over medium heat. Add diced pancetta or guanciale and sauté until it becomes crispy and golden.

Prepare Sauce Mixture:
- In a bowl, whisk together the eggs, grated Pecorino Romano, Parmesan, and a generous amount of freshly ground black pepper. Mix until well combined.

Combine Pasta and Sauce:
- Once the pasta is cooked, reserve a cup of pasta water, then drain the rest. Immediately toss the hot pasta with the cooked pancetta or guanciale in the skillet. The heat from the pasta will partially cook the eggs in the next step.

Add Sauce Mixture:
- Remove the skillet from heat and quickly pour the egg and cheese mixture over the pasta. Toss the pasta rapidly to coat it evenly. If the sauce is too thick, add a bit of the reserved pasta water gradually until you achieve a creamy consistency.

Serve Immediately:
- Serve the Carbonara immediately, garnished with additional black pepper and grated cheese if desired.

Authentic Carbonara is simple and relies on the quality of its ingredients. The key is to work quickly once you combine the pasta and sauce to create a creamy and velvety texture without scrambling the eggs. Enjoy this classic Roman dish as a delightful taste of Italian cuisine!

Greek Spanakopita (Spinach Pie)

Ingredients:

For the Filling:

- 1 pound (450g) fresh spinach, washed and chopped
- 1 cup feta cheese, crumbled
- 1 cup ricotta cheese
- 1 cup green onions, finely chopped
- 3 large eggs, lightly beaten
- 1/4 cup fresh dill, chopped
- 1/4 cup fresh parsley, chopped
- Salt and pepper to taste
- Olive oil for sautéing

For the Phyllo Dough:

- 1 package (16 ounces) phyllo dough, thawed according to package instructions
- 1 cup unsalted butter, melted

Instructions:

Prepare the Spinach:
- In a large skillet, heat a drizzle of olive oil over medium heat. Add the chopped spinach and sauté until wilted. Allow the excess liquid to drain and cool.

Prepare the Filling:
- In a large mixing bowl, combine the wilted spinach, crumbled feta cheese, ricotta cheese, chopped green onions, beaten eggs, fresh dill, fresh parsley, salt, and pepper. Mix well to ensure an even distribution of ingredients.

Assemble the Spanakopita:
- Preheat the oven to 350°F (175°C). Brush a baking dish with melted butter.
- Carefully unroll the phyllo dough and place it between two slightly damp kitchen towels to prevent drying out.

- Lay one sheet of phyllo dough in the prepared baking dish, brush it lightly with melted butter, and repeat with about 7-8 layers.
- Spread half of the spinach and cheese filling evenly over the phyllo layers.
- Continue layering the remaining phyllo sheets on top of the filling, brushing each layer with melted butter.
- Spread the remaining filling over the final layer of phyllo.
- Fold any excess phyllo edges over the top, and brush the top layer with additional melted butter.

Bake:
- Bake in the preheated oven for about 45-50 minutes or until the Spanakopita is golden brown and crisp.

Cool and Serve:
- Allow the Spanakopita to cool for a few minutes before slicing into squares or triangles. Serve warm or at room temperature.

Greek Spanakopita is a delightful appetizer or side dish, perfect for gatherings and celebrations. The combination of flaky phyllo dough and the flavorful spinach and cheese filling creates a dish that is both satisfying and delicious.

Vietnamese Egg Coffee

Ingredients:

For the Egg Cream:

- 2 large eggs
- 4 tablespoons condensed milk
- 2 tablespoons sugar (optional, adjust to taste)

For the Coffee:

- 2 tablespoons coarsely ground Vietnamese or dark roast coffee
- 1 cup hot water

Instructions:

Prepare the Coffee:
- Brew a strong cup of Vietnamese or dark roast coffee using your preferred method. You can use a drip filter, French press, or any other coffee brewing method you have.

Make the Egg Cream:
- In a bowl, whisk together the egg yolks, condensed milk, and sugar (if using) until the mixture is well combined and slightly thickened.

Whip the Egg Cream:
- Using a hand mixer or a whisk, beat the egg mixture until it becomes fluffy and has a pale yellow color. This usually takes about 5-7 minutes of whisking.

Assemble the Vietnamese Egg Coffee:
- Pour the hot brewed coffee into a mug.
- Spoon the whipped egg cream on top of the coffee. You can either spoon it gently to float on top or pour it in the center for a more layered presentation.

Serve and Enjoy:
- Serve the Vietnamese Egg Coffee immediately while it's still warm.

Optional: Add Ice (for Iced Egg Coffee):

- If you prefer iced coffee, let the coffee cool to room temperature and then refrigerate until cold. Pour it over ice and top with the whipped egg cream.

Vietnamese Egg Coffee is a delightful combination of strong coffee and the creamy sweetness of the egg mixture. It's a popular and indulgent treat in Vietnam, and making it at home allows you to experience this unique coffee creation. Enjoy the rich and velvety texture of Vietnamese Egg Coffee!

Mexican Chiles Rellenos

Ingredients:

For the Filling:

- 4 large poblano peppers (or Anaheim peppers)
- 1 cup shredded Monterey Jack cheese or Oaxaca cheese
- 1 cup cooked and seasoned ground beef or shredded chicken (optional)
- 1/2 cup finely chopped onion
- 1 garlic clove, minced
- Salt and pepper to taste

For the Batter:

- 4 large eggs, separated
- 1/2 cup all-purpose flour
- 1/2 teaspoon baking powder
- Salt to taste

For Frying:

- Vegetable oil for frying

For the Sauce:

- 2 cups tomato sauce
- 1 garlic clove, minced
- 1 teaspoon dried oregano
- 1 teaspoon ground cumin
- Salt and pepper to taste

Instructions:

Roast and Peel the Peppers:
- Roast the poblano peppers over an open flame, on a grill, or under a broiler until the skin is charred and blistered. Place them in a plastic bag or covered bowl for 10-15 minutes to steam, making it easier to peel the skin. Peel, remove seeds, and set aside.

Prepare the Filling:

- In a skillet, sauté the chopped onion and minced garlic until softened. Add the seasoned ground beef or shredded chicken (if using) and cook until browned. Season with salt and pepper. Remove from heat and let it cool.

Stuff the Peppers:
- Stuff each roasted and peeled pepper with a mixture of shredded cheese and the cooked filling.

Prepare the Batter:
- In a bowl, whisk the egg whites until stiff peaks form. In a separate bowl, whisk the egg yolks, flour, baking powder, and salt until well combined. Gently fold in the beaten egg whites.

Batter and Fry the Peppers:
- Dip each stuffed pepper into the batter, ensuring it's fully coated. Fry in hot vegetable oil until golden brown on all sides. Place on a paper towel to drain excess oil.

Make the Sauce:
- In a saucepan, combine tomato sauce, minced garlic, dried oregano, ground cumin, salt, and pepper. Simmer for 10-15 minutes until the flavors meld.

Serve:
- Pour the sauce over the Chiles Rellenos before serving.

Chiles Rellenos are often served with rice and beans or a side of Mexican crema. Enjoy these delicious and flavorful stuffed peppers as a classic Mexican dish!

Cajun Shrimp and Grits with a Fried Egg

Ingredients:

For the Grits:

- 1 cup stone-ground grits
- 4 cups water or chicken broth
- 1 cup sharp cheddar cheese, shredded
- Salt and black pepper to taste
- 2 tablespoons butter

For the Cajun Shrimp:

- 1 pound large shrimp, peeled and deveined
- 2 tablespoons Cajun seasoning (store-bought or homemade)
- 2 tablespoons olive oil
- 3 cloves garlic, minced
- 1 tablespoon fresh lemon juice
- Salt and black pepper to taste
- Chopped fresh parsley for garnish

For the Fried Eggs:

- 4 eggs
- Salt and black pepper to taste
- Cooking spray or butter for frying

Instructions:

Prepare the Grits:
- In a medium saucepan, bring the water or chicken broth to a boil. Slowly whisk in the grits, reduce heat to low, cover, and simmer. Stir occasionally until the grits are creamy and tender, about 20-25 minutes.
- Once the grits are cooked, stir in the shredded cheddar cheese, butter, salt, and black pepper. Keep warm.

Cajun Shrimp:

- In a bowl, toss the peeled and deveined shrimp with Cajun seasoning, minced garlic, fresh lemon juice, salt, and black pepper.
- Heat olive oil in a large skillet over medium-high heat. Add the seasoned shrimp and cook for 2-3 minutes per side or until they turn pink and opaque. Remove from heat.

Fried Eggs:
- In a separate pan, heat cooking spray or butter over medium heat. Crack the eggs into the pan, keeping the yolks intact. Season with salt and black pepper. Fry until the edges are crispy, and the yolks are cooked to your liking.

Assemble the Dish:
- Divide the creamy grits among serving plates. Top each plate with a portion of Cajun shrimp. Place a fried egg on top of the shrimp.
- Garnish with chopped fresh parsley and additional black pepper if desired.

Serve:
- Serve the Cajun Shrimp and Grits with a Fried Egg immediately, allowing the yolk to run over the dish.

This dish is a delightful combination of textures and flavors, with creamy grits, spicy shrimp, and a luscious fried egg. Enjoy this Southern comfort food for a satisfying and flavorful meal!

Egyptian Ful Medames with Egg

Ingredients:

For the Ful Medames:

- 1 cup dried fava beans
- 3 cloves garlic, minced
- 1/4 cup fresh lemon juice
- 2 tablespoons olive oil
- 1 teaspoon ground cumin
- Salt to taste
- Chopped fresh parsley for garnish (optional)

For the Eggs:

- 4 eggs
- Salt and black pepper to taste
- Olive oil or butter for frying or poaching

Instructions:

Prepare the Fava Beans:
- Rinse the dried fava beans and soak them in water overnight. The next day, drain and rinse the beans.
- In a large pot, cover the soaked fava beans with water and bring to a boil. Reduce heat to a simmer and cook until the beans are tender, about 1-2 hours. You can also use canned fava beans, which will significantly reduce the cooking time.

Season the Ful Medames:
- Drain the cooked fava beans and transfer them to a bowl. Add minced garlic, fresh lemon juice, olive oil, ground cumin, and salt. Mash the beans with a fork or a potato masher until you achieve a coarse texture.
- Adjust the seasoning to your taste.

Prepare the Eggs:
- In a separate pan, heat olive oil or butter over medium heat. Fry or poach the eggs to your liking. Season with salt and black pepper.

Assemble the Dish:

- Divide the Ful Medames among serving plates, creating a well in the center. Place a fried or poached egg in the well.
- Garnish with chopped fresh parsley if desired.

Serve:
- Serve the Egyptian Ful Medames with Egg immediately, accompanied by flatbread or pita on the side.

This dish is not only delicious but also nutritious and protein-packed. It's a popular breakfast or brunch option in Egypt, and the addition of the egg adds richness and extra flavor. Enjoy your Egyptian Ful Medames with a perfectly cooked egg!

Lebanese Eggplant and Egg Casserole (Batenjan Mehsheh)

Ingredients:

- 2 large eggplants, sliced into 1/2-inch rounds
- Salt for sweating eggplants
- Olive oil for brushing eggplants and greasing the baking dish
- 1 large onion, finely chopped
- 3 cloves garlic, minced
- 4 large tomatoes, diced
- 1/4 cup tomato paste
- 1 teaspoon ground cumin
- 1 teaspoon ground coriander
- 1/2 teaspoon ground cinnamon
- Salt and black pepper to taste
- 4-6 eggs (depending on the size of your baking dish)
- Fresh parsley, chopped, for garnish

Instructions:

Prepare the Eggplants:
- Sprinkle salt on both sides of the eggplant slices and let them sweat for about 20-30 minutes. Rinse and pat dry.
- Preheat the oven to 375°F (190°C).
- Brush the eggplant slices with olive oil and arrange them on a baking sheet. Roast in the preheated oven for about 15-20 minutes or until they are tender and lightly browned. Set aside.

Make the Tomato Sauce:
- In a large skillet, heat olive oil over medium heat. Add chopped onions and sauté until they become translucent.
- Add minced garlic and continue sautéing for another minute.
- Add diced tomatoes, tomato paste, ground cumin, ground coriander, ground cinnamon, salt, and black pepper. Cook until the tomatoes break down and the sauce thickens.

Layer the Casserole:
- Grease a baking dish with olive oil. Place a layer of roasted eggplant slices at the bottom of the dish.

- Spoon a portion of the tomato sauce over the eggplant layer. Repeat the process, alternating between eggplant and tomato sauce, until you run out of ingredients, finishing with a layer of tomato sauce on top.

Crack and Add the Eggs:
- Make small wells in the tomato sauce and crack an egg into each well.
- Bake in the preheated oven for about 15-20 minutes or until the egg whites are set, but the yolks are still runny.

Garnish and Serve:
- Garnish the Lebanese Eggplant and Egg Casserole with chopped fresh parsley.
- Serve the casserole hot, straight from the baking dish.

This Lebanese dish offers a delightful combination of flavors, with the roasted eggplants providing a smoky touch to the tomato and egg layers. It's a comforting and satisfying casserole that can be enjoyed for brunch, lunch, or dinner.

Dutch Baby Pancake with Lemon and Powdered Sugar

Ingredients:

- 3 large eggs
- 2/3 cup all-purpose flour
- 2/3 cup milk
- 1 tablespoon granulated sugar
- 1/2 teaspoon vanilla extract
- 1/4 teaspoon salt
- 3 tablespoons unsalted butter
- Powdered sugar, for dusting
- Lemon wedges, for serving

Instructions:

Preheat the Oven:
- Preheat your oven to 425°F (220°C). Place a 10-inch ovenproof skillet or cast-iron pan in the oven while it preheats.

Prepare the Batter:
- In a blender, combine the eggs, flour, milk, granulated sugar, vanilla extract, and salt. Blend until smooth.

Heat the Skillet:
- Carefully remove the hot skillet from the oven. Add the butter, swirling it around to coat the bottom and sides of the pan as it melts.

Bake the Pancake:
- Quickly pour the batter into the hot skillet with melted butter. Place the skillet back into the preheated oven.
- Bake for about 20-25 minutes or until the pancake is puffed up and golden brown around the edges.

Serve:
- Remove the Dutch Baby Pancake from the oven. It will deflate slightly as it cools.
- Squeeze fresh lemon juice over the pancake and dust generously with powdered sugar.
- Serve immediately, cut into wedges, with additional lemon wedges on the side.

Optional Toppings:

- You can add other toppings like fresh berries, whipped cream, or a drizzle of maple syrup if desired.

The Dutch Baby Pancake with Lemon and Powdered Sugar is a show-stopping breakfast treat. The crispy edges and soft, custardy center make it a delightful and easy-to-make option for a special morning. Enjoy!

Egg and Vegetable Stir-Fry

Ingredients:

- 4 large eggs
- 2 tablespoons soy sauce
- 1 tablespoon oyster sauce
- 1 tablespoon cornstarch
- 1 tablespoon water
- 2 tablespoons vegetable oil
- 1 cup broccoli florets
- 1 bell pepper, thinly sliced
- 1 carrot, julienned
- 1 cup snap peas, ends trimmed
- 2 green onions, sliced (white and green parts separated)
- 2 cloves garlic, minced
- 1 teaspoon grated ginger
- Cooked rice or noodles for serving

Instructions:

Prepare the Sauce:
- In a small bowl, whisk together soy sauce, oyster sauce, cornstarch, and water. Set aside.

Whisk the Eggs:
- In a separate bowl, whisk the eggs. Add a pinch of salt and pepper if desired.

Stir-Fry the Vegetables:
- Heat vegetable oil in a large wok or skillet over medium-high heat. Add broccoli, bell pepper, carrot, snap peas, and the white parts of green onions. Stir-fry for 3-4 minutes until the vegetables are slightly tender but still crisp.

Add Garlic and Ginger:
- Add minced garlic and grated ginger to the vegetables. Stir-fry for an additional 1-2 minutes until fragrant.

Push Vegetables to the Side:
- Push the vegetables to one side of the wok or skillet. Pour the whisked eggs into the empty side.

Cook the Eggs:
- Allow the eggs to set for a moment and then scramble them with a spatula. Cook until they are fully cooked but still moist.

Combine Eggs and Vegetables:
- Mix the cooked eggs with the stir-fried vegetables in the wok or skillet.

Add Sauce:
- Pour the prepared sauce over the egg and vegetable mixture. Stir to coat everything evenly.

Finish with Green Onions:
- Add the green parts of the sliced green onions. Stir for an additional 1-2 minutes until the sauce thickens and coats the ingredients.

Serve:
- Serve the Egg and Vegetable Stir-Fry over cooked rice or noodles.

Feel free to customize this recipe by adding your favorite vegetables or protein sources like tofu, chicken, or shrimp. Egg and Vegetable Stir-Fry is a versatile and delicious dish that can be enjoyed for a quick and satisfying meal.

Southwestern Breakfast Burrito

Ingredients:

- 4 large eggs
- 1 tablespoon olive oil
- 1/2 cup diced onion
- 1/2 cup diced bell pepper (any color)
- 1 cup black beans, cooked and drained
- 1 teaspoon ground cumin
- 1 teaspoon chili powder
- Salt and pepper to taste
- 1 cup shredded cheddar or Monterey Jack cheese
- 4 large flour tortillas
- Salsa, avocado, sour cream, and cilantro for serving (optional)

Instructions:

Cook the Eggs:
- In a bowl, whisk the eggs. Heat olive oil in a skillet over medium heat. Add diced onions and bell peppers. Sauté until softened.
- Pour the whisked eggs over the vegetables in the skillet. Scramble the eggs until fully cooked.

Add Black Beans and Spices:
- Stir in the cooked black beans, ground cumin, chili powder, salt, and pepper. Mix well to combine and heat through.

Assemble the Burritos:
- Warm the flour tortillas in the microwave or on a skillet for a few seconds.
- Spoon the egg and black bean mixture onto each tortilla. Sprinkle shredded cheese over the top.
- Optionally, add salsa, sliced avocado, sour cream, and fresh cilantro.

Fold the Burritos:
- Fold the sides of each tortilla towards the center, then fold the bottom up, and roll tightly to form a burrito.

Serve:
- Place the Southwestern Breakfast Burritos seam side down on a serving plate.
- Optionally, top with additional salsa, avocado, sour cream, and cilantro.

Enjoy:

- Serve the Southwestern Breakfast Burritos immediately, and enjoy your flavorful and satisfying breakfast.

Feel free to customize your Southwestern Breakfast Burrito with other ingredients like sautéed mushrooms, spinach, or diced tomatoes. This versatile recipe allows you to create a delicious breakfast that suits your taste preferences.

Caprese Egg Salad

Ingredients:

- 6 hard-boiled eggs, chopped
- 1 cup cherry tomatoes, halved
- 1 cup fresh mozzarella balls (bocconcini), halved
- 1/4 cup fresh basil leaves, chopped
- 2 tablespoons extra-virgin olive oil
- 1 tablespoon balsamic glaze (or balsamic vinegar)
- Salt and black pepper to taste

Instructions:

Prepare the Eggs:
- Hard boil the eggs, let them cool, and then peel and chop them.

Assemble the Salad:
- In a large mixing bowl, combine the chopped hard-boiled eggs, cherry tomatoes, fresh mozzarella balls, and chopped basil.

Dress the Salad:
- Drizzle extra-virgin olive oil and balsamic glaze (or balsamic vinegar) over the salad.

Season:
- Season the salad with salt and black pepper to taste.

Toss Gently:
- Gently toss all the ingredients together until well combined.

Chill (Optional):
- If desired, refrigerate the Caprese Egg Salad for about 30 minutes to allow the flavors to meld and the salad to chill.

Serve:
- Serve the Caprese Egg Salad on its own or on a bed of fresh greens, in a sandwich, or with crusty bread.

This Caprese Egg Salad is not only delicious but also visually appealing with its vibrant colors. The combination of eggs, tomatoes, mozzarella, and basil creates a refreshing and satisfying dish. Enjoy it as a light lunch, brunch, or a side dish at your next gathering!

Smoky Deviled Eggs

Ingredients:

- 6 hard-boiled eggs
- 3 tablespoons mayonnaise
- 1 teaspoon Dijon mustard
- 1 teaspoon smoked paprika
- 1/2 teaspoon liquid smoke (adjust to taste)
- Salt and pepper, to taste
- Chopped chives or parsley for garnish (optional)

Instructions:

Hard-Boil Eggs: Place the eggs in a saucepan and cover with water. Bring the water to a boil, then reduce the heat to a simmer and cook for about 10 minutes. Remove from heat, cool, and peel the eggs.

Slice and Scoop: Cut the hard-boiled eggs in half lengthwise. Carefully remove the yolks and place them in a bowl. Arrange the egg white halves on a serving platter.

Make Filling: Mash the egg yolks with a fork. Add mayonnaise, Dijon mustard, smoked paprika, liquid smoke, salt, and pepper. Mix until smooth and well combined. Adjust seasonings to taste.

Fill the Eggs: Spoon or pipe the yolk mixture back into the egg white halves. You can use a pastry bag for a more decorative look.

Garnish: Sprinkle additional smoked paprika on top for extra smokiness. Garnish with chopped chives or parsley if desired.

Chill: Refrigerate the deviled eggs for at least 30 minutes before serving to allow the flavors to meld.

Serve: Arrange the smoky deviled eggs on a serving platter and enjoy!

Feel free to adjust the ingredients to suit your taste preferences. These smoky deviled eggs are a flavorful twist on the classic recipe, perfect for appetizers or party snacks.

Japanese Tamagoyaki (Sweet Rolled Omelette)

Ingredients:

- 4 large eggs
- 2 tablespoons sugar
- 1 tablespoon soy sauce
- 1 tablespoon mirin (sweet rice wine)
- 1/2 teaspoon salt
- 1/2 teaspoon dashi powder (optional, for added flavor)
- 1 tablespoon vegetable oil (for greasing the pan)

Instructions:

Prepare Ingredients: In a bowl, whisk together the eggs, sugar, soy sauce, mirin, salt, and dashi powder until well combined.

Strain Mixture: Strain the egg mixture through a fine mesh sieve to ensure a smooth and silky texture for the tamagoyaki.

Preheat Pan: Heat a rectangular tamagoyaki pan or a regular non-stick skillet over medium heat. Brush the pan with a thin layer of vegetable oil using a paper towel or a brush.

Pour a Thin Layer: Pour a thin layer of the egg mixture into the pan, tilting it to spread the mixture evenly. As the edges set, gently roll the egg layer from one end of the pan to the other using chopsticks or a spatula.

Oil the Empty Space: Before adding another layer, lift the rolled egg and apply a bit more oil to the empty space in the pan. Pour in another thin layer of the egg mixture, making sure it flows under the rolled egg.

Roll and Repeat: Once the new layer starts to set, roll it up to the existing rolled egg. Repeat this process, adding layers and rolling until all the egg mixture is used.

Shape the Omelette: Use a bamboo sushi rolling mat or the edge of the pan to shape the tamagoyaki into a neat rectangle. Keep rolling until you reach the end of the pan.

Cool and Slice: Allow the tamagoyaki to cool slightly before slicing it into bite-sized pieces. This can be done with a sharp knife, wiping it with a paper towel between cuts for a cleaner finish.

Serve: Arrange the sliced tamagoyaki on a plate and serve as a side dish or on its own. It's delicious both warm and at room temperature.

Tamagoyaki makes a delightful addition to bento boxes, sushi platters, or as a tasty snack. Enjoy your sweet rolled omelette!